AL-MIʿRAJIYYA

Also available:

Abdal Hakim Murad (ed.), *Turkish Sacred Songs*, ISBN 978 1 902350 12 7.
Husayn Vaiz Kashifi, *Gleams from the Rawdat al-Shuhada*, ISBN 978 1 902350 11 0.
Abdal Hakim Murad, *Al-Hamdiyya*. ISBN 978 1 902350 13 4.
Abdal Hakim Murad, *Muslim Songs of the British Isles*. ISBN 1 872038 14 X.

ترتيب اشعار واذكار

المعراجية

على اصول القلادنة

AL-MIʿRAJIYYA

Prepared for Recital
by Abdal Hakim Murad

MUSLIM ACADEMIC TRUST

The Muslim Academic Trust
14 St Paul's Road
Cambridge CB1 2EZ
United Kingdom

ISBN 978 1 902350 15 8
www.muslimacademictrust.org

This book is sold in support of
the Cambridge Central Mosque

PRINTED IN THE UNITED KINGDOM BY BIDDLES BOOKS LTD

Contents

بسم الله الرحمن الرحيم

Introduction

THIS BOOK ATTEMPTS to provide a first appearance in the English language of a distinctive and much-loved genre of Muslim literature. The Ascension of the Prophet ﷺ, often seen as the culminating event of his life, is a story which carries within itself a wide range of characteristically Islamic themes. Down the centuries it has inspired scholars and poets to reanimate the hearts of their listeners by rehearsing its great concerns, and it is to be hoped that this same reanimation will be possible today in our Anglophone context.

The earliest Muslim historians recorded the events of the Ascension in some detail. During the most difficult period of his ministry in Mecca, the Holy Prophet was miraculously taken on a night journey (*isrā'*) from the Meccan sanctuary to the sanctuary of Jerusalem. Here he prayed with some of the prophets of earlier ages, after which he experienced an ascension (*mi'rāj*) as he was carried up by the Angel Gabriel through the seven heavens into the Divine Presence.

The story allows the hearer to recall some principles which are integral to Islam's place in the history of religion. The Meccan Sanctuary, the 'first worshipping-place of mankind', is connected to the holy location which is now the Al-Aqsa Mosque, which following the arrival of the multi-ethnic Islamic community became the 'house of prayer for all nations' foretold in the Gospels, and which remains the third holiest pilgrimage destination in Islam. In this place, the Prophet ﷺ affirms and prays with Jesus, John, Abraham, Moses and other great figures of the earlier monotheisms, thus signalling that Islam's appearance is a moment of inclusion and embrace, as the scripture tells us: 'We make no distinction between any of His messengers.' (2:136)

The Prophet's ﷺ subsequent ascent through the 'seven heavens', whose true nature evidently defies exact accounting, also shows him as affirming and embracing the earlier prophets. At last he reaches the mysterious Lote

Tree and the degree of Two Bows' Lengths, where 'the heart did not falsify that which it saw' (53:11). After this ultimate spiritual encounter with the One Lord, he retraces his journey, bearing several gifts, one of which is the five-fold prayer which to this day is incumbent upon all followers of his way.

From the earliest times Muslim scholars strove to conserve the hadith narrations which preserved the memory of this decisive event. There are long accounts in the anthologies of al-Bukhārī and Muslim, which have served as the basis for the present volume. Qur'anic commentaries also furnished additional details when dealing with the relevant verses.

The classical poets of Islam loved to incorporate sections describing the Ascension within their longer works; these included Sanā'ī (d.1140), Niẓāmī (d.1209), 'Aṭṭār (d.1221), and Jāmī (d.1492). In addition, scholars and poets composed innumerable works dedicated exclusively to the subject, some of which were succinct, while others became long and very elaborate. The philosopher Ibn Sīnā (d.1037) wrote a *Me'rāj-nāme (Book of the Mi'rāj)* to explore the story's metaphysical significance, while his Sufi contemporary al-Qushayrī (d.1072), perhaps in response, wrote a non-philosophical *Kitāb al-Mi'rāj* in which he celebrated the story as a classic narrative of spiritual ascent from the shadows of our world, through intermediary levels of being, to the One. Perhaps the most popular text in the Arabic world was the *Qiṣṣat al-Mi'rāj* (*Mi'rāj Story*) of Ja'far al-Barzanjī (d.1764), a celebrated Shāfi'ī mufti of Madina. This text, which exists also in Swahili translation, is still widely and enthusiastically recited at gatherings. Elsewhere in Africa there are *Mi'rājiyyas* in languages such as Peul, Fulani and Wolof.

In the Persian language, scholars and saints also composed a large number of Mi'rāj works, some of which were in prose, while others took the form either of verse or a medley of prose and poetry. Among the best-known were works by Aḥmed Aflākī (1360), Tāj al-Din Aḥmedī (d.1412), Jamāl al-Din 'Alavī (d.1590), and 'Alī Nabṭīnī (d.1650). Many Indian writers also celebrated the same subject, in a long literary tradition which extended from Ḥamīd al-Din Nāgūrī (d.1274?) to Muḥammad Idrīs Kāndahlawī (d.1974) and beyond.

In the Turkic languages the process seems to have begun with the Central Asian poet Ḥakīm Atā (d.1186), followed by many others, reaching a peak in the eighteenth century Ottoman world. One very popular Ascension book was written by Ismā'īl Ḥaqqī Bursevī (d.1725), whose text is still reprinted regularly. The most artistically elaborate was by the Bosnian poet Ṣābit (d.1712). Many regard the text of Ġanī-zāde Meḥmed Nādirī (d.1627) as the finest in Turkish; this was the work of a chief religious judge of the Ottoman Balkans, whose work was emulated by several later poets. ʿAbdülbāqī ʿĀrif (d.1713), was a madrasa director in Istanbul and a chief inspector of the charitable endowments *(awqāf)* in Mecca and Madina; his text was recited at the Eyüp mosque in Istanbul annually for many years. In the twentieth century another *Miʿrājiyya* (*Miraciye*) was authored by Fatima Kamile Hanım (d.1921).

To educate the broader population about the Ascension, Islamic cultures evolved forms of ceremonial recital. These varied very considerably. In the Ottoman universe, for example, the date of the *Miʿrāj*, the 27th of the month of Rajab, was commemorated by specialized reciters known as *miʿrāc-ḫān*, who might be financially supported by a *waqf* endowment established specifically for this purpose. Often two such reciters sitting on elevated chairs (*kursī*) would preside in the larger mosques, taking it in turns to sing the text, using the rhythms and modes of classical Ottoman oral culture, while the congregation joined in the chorus. At the key moment where the Prophet ﷺ is offered a goblet of wine and a goblet of milk, and chooses the latter, cups of milk might be passed around for the audience to drink. These traditions are currently enjoying a renaissance in Turkey. Related customs are traditional throughout the Muslim world, notably in Egypt, East Africa, and Indonesia. Particularly notable is the annual recital at the Kensington mosque in Cape Town, broadcast live on local radio.

The present work, entitled simply *al-Miʿrājiyya*, follows the traditional sequence mapped out originally by the hadith literature and subsequently developed for public artistic recitation by religious scholars and cantors. Containing sung and spoken elements, it is designed for recital by a small group of vocalists (with the congregation joining in *ad lib*), and is intended only as a general guide, as improvisation lies at the heart of this tradition. The tunes are adapted from familiar Celtic folk melodies, as classical Middle Eastern and Indian singing, with its complex rhythms and its system of modes and microtones, can be difficult for Muslims in the West to master easily, and can be challenging also for audiences. However, free rhythms and microtones are not unfamiliar to the *sean nós* and other traditions of *a capella* song present in the Gaelic world, and some vocalists may wish to experiment with this convergence, which is reflective perhaps of other deep historical links between Europe's Atlantic fringe and the Middle East, visible, as is often noted, in the flowing decorative motifs of the *Book of Kells*. It is also pleasing to note that the Celtic open-ended drum, the *bodhrán*, is very similar to equivalents in the Islamic world such as the *daff* and the *bendir,* and can be played in a similar way, with one hand controlling timbre and pitch.

It is hoped that this modest effort will help to engage audiences brought up in the West with the timeless and beautiful story of the Prophetic Ascension.

ABDAL HAKIM MURAD

بِسۡمِ ٱللَّهِ ٱلرَّحۡمَٰنِ ٱلرَّحِيمِ ١

ٱلۡحَمۡدُ لِلَّهِ رَبِّ ٱلۡعَٰلَمِينَ ٢

ٱلرَّحۡمَٰنِ ٱلرَّحِيمِ ٣

مَٰلِكِ يَوۡمِ ٱلدِّينِ ٤

إِيَّاكَ نَعۡبُدُ وَإِيَّاكَ نَسۡتَعِينُ ٥

ٱهۡدِنَا ٱلصِّرَٰطَ ٱلۡمُسۡتَقِيمَ ٦

صِرَٰطَ ٱلَّذِينَ أَنۡعَمۡتَ عَلَيۡهِمۡ غَيۡرِ
ٱلۡمَغۡضُوبِ عَلَيۡهِمۡ وَلَا ٱلضَّآلِّينَ ٧

بِسۡمِ ٱللَّهِ ٱلرَّحۡمَٰنِ ٱلرَّحِيمِ

سُبۡحَٰنَ ٱلَّذِيٓ أَسۡرَىٰ بِعَبۡدِهِۦ لَيۡلٗا مِّنَ
ٱلۡمَسۡجِدِ ٱلۡحَرَامِ إِلَى ٱلۡمَسۡجِدِ ٱلۡأَقۡصَا
ٱلَّذِي بَٰرَكۡنَا حَوۡلَهُۥ لِنُرِيَهُۥ مِنۡ ءَايَٰتِنَآۚ
إِنَّهُۥ هُوَ ٱلسَّمِيعُ ٱلۡبَصِيرُ ١

صَدَقَ اللّٰهُ العَظِيم

بِسْمِ اللهِ الرَّحْمٰنِ الرَّحِيم
وَالصَّلاَةُ وَالسَّلاَمُ عَلَى أَكْرَمِ الأَنْبِيَاءِ وَالمُرْسَلِينَ
سَيِّدِنَا وَمَولاَنَا حَضْرَةِ مُحَمَّدٍ قَايِدِ الغُرِّ المُحَجَّلِينَ
اِصْطَفَاهُ رَبُّهُ وَآدَمُ بَيْنَ المَاءِ والطِّينِ
ثُمَّ مِنْ جُودِهِ أَرْسَلَهُ رَحْمَةً لِلْعَالَمِينَ
وَلِعِظَمِ خُلُقِهِ أَلْقَى عَلَيهِ الفُرْقَانَ وَيٰسِينِ
صَاحِبِ الكَمَالاَتِ البَشَرِيَّةِ مَعْروفٍ بِاللُّطْفِ وَاللِّينِ
صَاحِبِ الجَمَالِ البَاهِرِ مَلاَذِ الوَرَى يومَ الدِّين

اللّٰهُمَّ نَسْأَلُكَ الأَجْرَ والقَبُولَ
وَتَمَامَ كُلِّ سُولٍ وَمَأْمُولٍ
فَتَقَبَّلْ مَا نَتْلُوهُ يَا خَيرَ مَسؤُول
وَأَبْلِغْنَا المَأْوَى بِحُبِّ الرَّسُول

سَلَامٌ قَوْلًا مِنْ رَبٍّ رَحِيمٍ (3 times)

Al-tahiyyātu li'llāhi al-zākiyyātu li'llāhi al-ṭayyibātu'ṣ-ṣalawātu li'Llāh. As-salāmu 'alayka ayyuha'n-nabiyyu wa-raḥmatu'Llāhi wa-barakātuh. As-salāmu 'alaynā wa-'alā 'ibādillāhi'ṣ-ṣāliḥīn. Ashhadu an lā ilāha illa'Llāh wa-ashhadu anna Muḥammadan 'abduhu wa-rasūluh

التَّحِيَّاتُ لِلّٰهِ الزَّاكِيَّاتُ لِلّٰهِ الطَّيِّبَاتُ الصَّلَوَاتُ لِلّٰهِ السَّلَامُ عَلَيْكَ أَيُّهَا النَّبِيُّ وَرَحْمَةُ اللهِ وَبَرَكَاتُهُ السَّلَامُ عَلَينَا وَعَلَى عِبَادِ اللهِ الصَّالِحِينَ أَشْهَدُ أَنْ لَا إِلٰهَ إِلَّا اللهُ وَحْدَهُ لَا شَرِيكَ لَهُ وَأَشْهَدُ أَنَّ مُحَمَّدًا عَبْدُهُ وَرَسُولُهُ

Nightingale of Purity!

عندليب الصفا

Tune: A ghaoil, leig dhachaigh gum mhàthair mi

صَلُّوا عَلَى المُصْطَفَى   كَذا آلِهِ الأَصْفَى
رَبُّهُ بِهِ أَسْرَى   نَالَ جَنَّةَ المَأْوَى

Ṣallū ʻala'l-Muṣṭafā, kadhā ālihi'l-aṣfā
Rabbuhu bihi asrā, nāla jannata'l-ma'wā

Nightingale of purity! In your rosy bower sing.
Lift your voice, make glad our hearts, in your verdant garden sing.

Dove, come hither, sound your song, sing His name, the time is Spring!
Thrilling to the lyre-bird's lay, buds are blowing in the Spring.

Birds that nest in Sidra tree, may we hear the news you bring?
Grant to us mere mortal men news of our eternal King!

We poor churls in this poor world, to our paltry pleasures cling,
How we yearn to understand, gentle birds, the song you sing.

Oh I faint, I am not well, in my heart I find a sting.
Would that I could seek the scent softly spread by beating wing.

Parrot, peacock, turtle dove; birds that all are worshipping,
Teach me that your song is love, of the Beauty of that King.

Surely does my spirit know that to Truth it's travelling
Must by love of Beauty go, else be veiled by every thing.

In this wisdom did the One Who from nothing all did bring,
Ken the spirits of mankind, for the best in witnessing.

Saw that Aḥmad's heart did love, purity most cherishing,
Love's keen knife had cleft his heart, beauty all-encompassing.

Adam still 'twixt clay and water of Heaven's fashioning,
Yet Ṭāhā a prophet was, to His oneness witnessing.

Harmony his character, in his humours balancing,
In his flesh compounded e'er soul and body worshipping.

Surely souls that are so clear, cadences of love will bring
The Beloved of the world to the hearts in witnessing.

Since the Light of earth and heaven's the name of Heaven's King,
It was meet the Man of Light held the right of witnessing.

Thus 'his eye would never swerve', as he rode on Burāq's wing,
For to see 'the greatest sign', of the secrets of his King.

The Shining Realm

Call to mind, my brethren dear, how once our Lord a Garden made,
Out from naught He beauty wrought, silver stream by vernal glade.

There His Names were woven true, all His qualities arrayed,
Peace supernal in each flower, unity in full displayed.

Let your hearts recall that joy, let His verses gift your aid,
May the oracle of God, Heaven's voice, your heart pervade.

Lordly speech calls this to mind: we in peace dwelt, undismayed;
Never in the vale of veiling, safe in Heaven's palisade.

Scripture tells of Ṭūbā tree, where the blessed sat in shade,
Safe they were from erring stain, minds from Maker never strayed.

But our distant parents fair to this lower world were weighed,
Of their seed some upright stayed; others heedlessness displayed.

But know this well: went they not down, to this world of lowest grade,
The Chosen One, of One the sign, had never led Love's cavalcade.

Al-taḥiyyātu li'llāhi al-zākiyyātu li'llāhi al-ṭayyibātu'ṣ-ṣalawātu li'Llāh.
As-salāmu ʿalayka ayyuha'n-nabiyyu wa-raḥmatu'Llāhi wa-barakātuh.
As-salāmu ʿalaynā wa-ʿalā ʿibādillāhi'ṣ-ṣāliḥīn. Ashhadu an lā ilāha
illa'Llāh wa-ashhadu anna Muḥammadan ʿabduhu wa-rasūluh

التَّحِيَّاتُ لِلّٰهِ الزَّاكِيَّاتُ لِلّٰهِ الطَّيِّبَاتُ الصَّلَوَاتُ لِلّٰهِ السَّلَامُ عَلَيْكَ أَيُّهَا النَّبِيُّ
وَرَحْمَةُ اللّٰهِ وَبَرَكَاتُهُ السَّلَامُ عَلَينَا وَعَلَى عِبَادِ اللّٰهِ الصَالِحِينَ أَشْهَدُ أَنْ لَا إِلٰهَ إِلَّا
اللّٰهُ وَحْدَهُ لَا شَرِيكَ لَهُ وَأَشْهَدُ أَنَّ مُحَمَّدًا عَبْدُهُ وَرَسُولُهُ

Adam's Descent

Listen now, you who gather here! In the earliest time, before there were times, the tent of Unity and Nearness was alone.

The subtlety of God's presence said this:
'Wait! Wait! Wait and see! We will uproot doubt, and strike envy down! We will take Adam the Chosen into the changeable abode by means of a slip. And the whole world shall hear that he is a prisoner there, distant and divided. But Our mysteries shall speak to his, with none to obstruct them. We will bring him a subtle chalice, and he will drink until his foes lie down in defeat. Although his tangible flesh shall submit to the Fall Down – *Ihbiṭū* (2:36) – his inner reality shall be entered into the citadel of grace. And what is this chalice of bliss from which he shall ever drink? It is this:

قُلْنَا ٱهْبِطُوا۟ مِنْهَا جَمِيعًا ۖ فَإِمَّا يَأْتِيَنَّكُم مِّنِّى هُدًى فَمَن تَبِعَ
هُدَاىَ فَلَا خَوْفٌ عَلَيْهِمْ وَلَا هُمْ يَحْزَنُونَ ﴿٣٨﴾

If guidance comes to you from Me, then those that follow Me, no fear shall be upon them, neither shall they grieve. (2:38).

How amazing a tale is this! To Adam it was said: Fall down! To Muṣṭafā it was said: Rise up! Adam, now enter the world so that the abode of clay may submit to the majesty of your rule! O Muḥammad! Arise to Paradise, so that the zenith of the spheres shall be beautified by your fair contemplation. The mystery is My saying: Fall down, to your father, so that I could say: Rise up! to you

Al-taḥiyyātu li'llāhi al-zākiyyātu li'llāhi al-ṭayyibātu'ṣ-ṣalawātu li'Llāh. As-salāmu ʿalayka ayyuha'n-nabiyyu wa-raḥmatu'Llāhi wa-barakātuh. As-salāmu ʿalaynā wa-ʿalā ʿibādillāhi'ṣ-ṣāliḥīn. Ashhadu an lā ilāha illa'Llāh wa-ashhadu anna Muḥammadan ʿabduhu wa-rasūluh

التَّحِيَّاتُ لِلَّهِ الزَّاكِيَّاتُ لِلَّهِ الطَّيِّبَاتُ الصَّلَوَاتُ لِلَّهِ السَّلَامُ عَلَيْكَ أَيُّهَا النَّبِيُّ
وَرَحْمَةُ اللهِ وَبَرَكَاتُهُ السَّلَامُ عَلَينَا وَعَلَى عِبَادِ اللهِ الصَّالِحِينَ أَشْهَدُ أَنْ لَا إِلٰهَ إِلَّا
اللهُ وَحْدَهُ لَا شَرِيكَ لَهُ وَأَشْهَدُ أَنَّ مُحَمَّدًا عَبْدُهُ وَرَسُولُهُ

The Prophetic Endurance

انشودة صبر النبي

صلى الله عليه وسلم

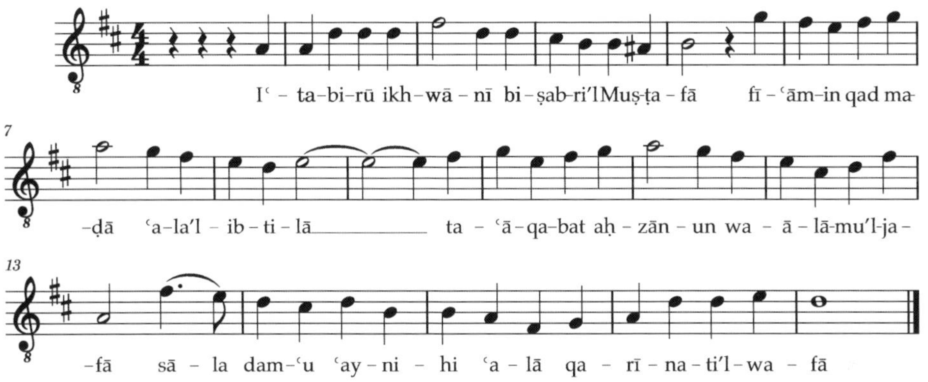

أُنْشُودَةُ صَبْرِ النَّبِي

صَلِّ رَبَّنَا عَلَى هذَا المُصْطَفَى
حَبِيبِ العَالَمِينَ كَنْزِ الصَّفَا
وَالآلِ وَالأَصْحَابِ وَكُلِّ مَنْ وَافَى
خَيْرِ سَادَةٍ وَقَادَةٍ أَقْطَابِ الإِقْتِفَاء

اِعْتَبِرُوا إِخْوَانِي بِصَبْرِ المُصْطَفَى   مِنْهُمْ زَكَرِيَّا وَالصَيفُ بِالقَفَا
فِي عَامٍ قَدْ مَضَى عَلَى الإِبْتِلَاء   وَنَجْلُ نُوحٍ هَدْيَهُ قَدْ نَفَا
تَعَاقَبَتْ أَحْزَانٌ وَآلَامُ الجَفَا   وَمُوسَى عِنْدَ هَزْلٍ بِرَبِّهِ اكْتَفَى
فَاضَ دَمْعُ عَيْنِهِ عَلَى قَرِينَةِ الوَفَا   قَومُ عِيسَى قَدْ نَالُوا مِنْهُ بِأَنْوَاعِ الجَفَا

مِنْ شَأْنِ الأَنْبِيَا أَهْلِ الصَّبْرِ وَالصَّفَا   جَاءَ الأَنْبِيَا بِالإِرْشَادِ وَالشِّفَا
مُكَابَدَةُ الجَحْدِ مِمَّنْ نَفَا   قُلُوبُهُمْ تَزَيَّنَتْ بِالوَفَا
أَشَدِّ النَّاسِ بَلْوَى وَضُرًّا لَمْ يَخْفَى   فَاللهُ مَعَ الصَّابِرِ جَهْرًا وَخَفَا
مِنْ مُعَانِدٍ وَمُنْكِرٍ وَأَجْلَافِ الجَفَا   حَتَّى جَاءَ خَتْمٌ لَهُمْ بِمَجِيءِ المُصْطَفَى

Tahlīl al-Qalādina

تهليل القلادنة

Tune: Omar Fraser

The Burāq

In the holy sanctuary, close by the Cube of Heaven, where the sky's night descends to this stony world, in the place of the remembrance of the First Covenant, in the habitation which lies straight beneath God's Throne, in the place where the Man of Praise, while still a boy, met angels who washed his heart with snow, bright in a golden grail, the prince of angels came again. He brought the Burāq, swift and bright as lightning, fair of face and bridled, a tall white beast of miracle, larger than a donkey and smaller than a mule. No earthly creature he, for with one leap his hooves could reach the limit of his gaze, and upon his legs were wings.

When the Chosen One made to mount him, he reared up. Art not ashamed, asked Gabriel, and laid his bright palm upon the creature's mane. By Allāh, you shall be ridden by he who is the dearest of all creatures to the Lord. And they say that the Burāq, on hearing this admonition, sweated copiously for shame, and remained quite still, so that the Chosen One could mount him. Those three lights shone in that deep darkness, in that time of sorrow and idol-love, in the desolate shrine of the one who saw three lights at the oak, in the year of sadness. Thus began the saga that we rehearse to you.

Al-taḥiyyātu li'llāhi al-zākiyyātu li'llāhi al-ṭayyibātu'ṣ-ṣalawātu li'Llāh.
As-salāmu ʿalayka ayyuha'n-nabiyyu wa-raḥmatu'Llāhi wa-barakātuh.
As-salāmu ʿalaynā wa-ʿalā ʿibādillāhi'ṣ-ṣāliḥīn. Ashhadu an lā ilāha
illa'Llāh wa-ashhadu anna Muḥammadan ʿabduhu wa-rasūluh

التَّحِيَّاتُ لِلَّهِ الزَّاكِيَّاتُ لِلَّهِ الطَّيِّبَاتُ الصَّلَوَاتُ لِلَّهِ السَّلَامُ عَلَيْكَ أَيُّهَا النَّبِيُّ
وَرَحْمَةُ اللهِ وَبَرَكَاتُهُ السَّلَامُ عَلَيْنَا وَعَلَى عِبَادِ اللهِ الصَّالِحِينَ أَشْهَدُ أَنْ لَا إِلَهَ إِلَّا
اللهُ وَحْدَهُ لَا شَرِيكَ لَهُ وَأَشْهَدُ أَنَّ مُحَمَّدًا عَبْدُهُ وَرَسُولُهُ

The Night Journey

اغنية الإسراء

Tune: Fill-iù Oro Hù Ò

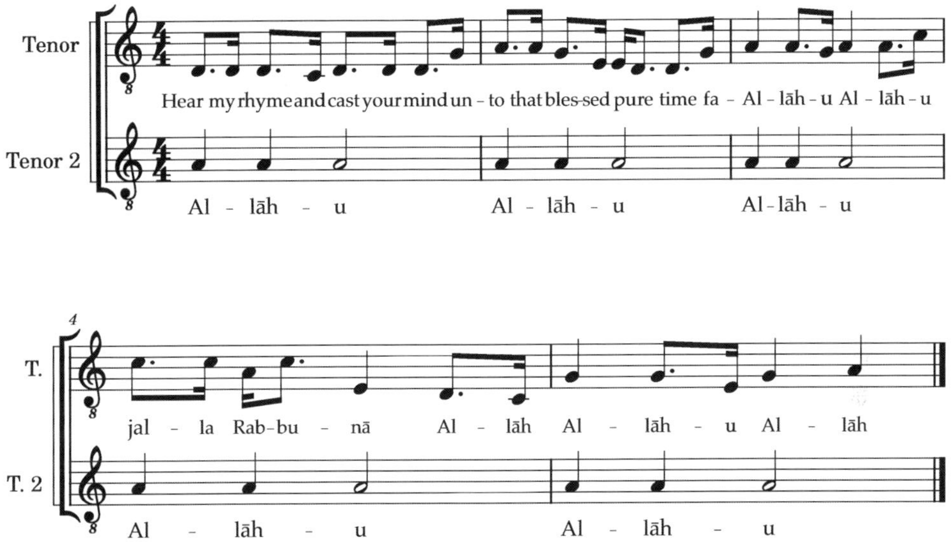

Fa-Allāhu Allāhu jalla rabbunā, Allāh Allāhu Allāh

Hear my rhyme and cast your mind unto that blessed pure time,
When by night the Maker's might revealed the House's birthright.
The city slept with all except the Man of Praise who prayer kept.
Heart awake for Heaven's sake he'd roads within the sky make.
Doves amazed, a trail he blazed, the angels called his name praised.
Mystery this history, our minds from such must needs flee.
Faithful flight he made by night and then beheld a tower bright.
Patriarchs had made their marks as did the maid of matriarchs.
All who there do stand in prayer a holy robe of grace wear.
Who denied ungodly pride shall find his wages multiplied.
Third of three in sanctity, for fruitfulness a palm-tree.
Stripped of life by Roman knife, that place of peace was all strife.
Halls that once heard Jesus pray, and shall again on Doomsday.
Isrāfīl the last appeal shall make and men shall all kneel.
Judgement-plain where all amain see hope and confidence wane.
Such a field, where Prophets kneeled, deserved to find a sure shield.
That abode which God bestowed a tyrant king its heart slowed.
That sanctuary did David see, but now did rot in pity.
Broken stone to God did moan, that earth had no more grace shown.
Purity, maturity, did languish in obscurity.
Till the cry that Aḥmad's nigh brought joy and made the hearts fly.
The ruined place, the Temple space, rejoiced to see his fair face.
Its duty to his beauty shown, a cry rose up from every stone.
See angels kneel to see the Seal whose beauty souls will unseal.
Idols fled, the angels said: the Temple rises from the dead.
His grace enfurled the ruined world, a shining future now whirled.

Jerusalem Encomia

المدائح المقدسية

Tune: O Cò Bheir Mi Leam

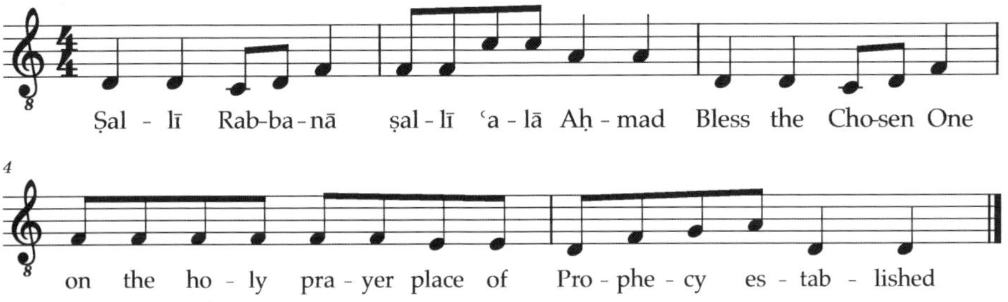

Ṣallī Rabbanā ṣallī ʿalā Aḥmad

Bless the Chosen One, on the holy prayer-place of Prophecy established.
Bless the Chosen One, set his foot upon the stone that Solomon established.
Bless the Chosen One, circled round by spirits of the Patriarchal sages.
Bless the Chosen One, blessed by all the noblest heroes of the elder ages.
Bless the Chosen One, hope of all the ages now in solemn adoration.
Bless the Chosen One, praying for the sorrows of the world in adulation.
Bless the Chosen One, raising up his blessed arms he calls on his Creator.
Bless the Chosen One, witness of the nations and the story's arbitrator.
Bless the Chosen One, stand before the worship lines and lead them all in praises.
Bless the Chosen One, Paraclete and Comforter, his light from Heaven blazes.
Bless the Chosen One, lifting high his blessed voice to lead the congregation.
Bless the Chosen One, one with all the Prophets as they make their attestation.
Bless the Chosen One, blessing them in unity and perfect adoration.
Bless the Chosen One, head of all the Prophets as they pray for our salvation.

Al-taḥiyyātu li'llāhi al-zākiyyātu li'llāhi al-ṭayyibātu'ṣ-ṣalawātu li'Llāh.
As-ṣalāmu ʿalayka ayyuha'n-nabiyyu wa-raḥmatu'Llāhi wa-barakātuh.
As-salāmu ʿalaynā wa-ʿalā ʿibādillāhi'ṣ-ṣāliḥīn. Ashhadu an lā ilāha
illa'Llāh wa-ashhadu anna Muḥammadan ʿabduhu wa-rasūluh

التَّحِيَّاتُ لِلهِ الزَّاكِيَّاتُ لِلهِ الطَّيِّبَاتُ الصَّلَوَاتُ لِلهِ السَّلَامُ عَلَيْكَ أَيُّهَا النَّبِيُّ
وَرَحْمَةُ اللهِ وَبَرَكَاتُهُ السَّلَامُ عَلَيْنَا وَعَلَى عِبَادِ اللهِ الصَّالِحِينَ أَشْهَدُ أَنْ لَا إِلٰهَ إِلَّا
اللهُ وَحْدَهُ لَا شَرِيكَ لَهُ وَأَشْهَدُ أَنَّ مُحَمَّدًا عَبْدُهُ وَرَسُولُهُ

Star of his Heartland

Star of his heartland
Crown of his kindred
Voyaged unhindered
Through darkling sky.
To the lost haven
Of Abram's story
Solomon's glory
Aḥmad did fly.

Ceased the old priesthood
Sacrifice ended
Sadducees wended
back to the tomb.
Court of the Gentiles
With Levites splendid
All now suspended
Matched to their doom.

Palace and prelate
In segmentation
By abjuration
metamorphose.
Ishmael has risen!
And his vocation
Unification
To the Land shows.

Years of Tears

أعوام الحزن

Tune: Unst Boat Song

24
T.
-wa-rā were the guer-don of his ef-fort ṣal – lī ʿa–lā Aḥ – mad
T.
Bar.
A
33
T.
2.Son of sor – rows sum of hardships ṣal – lī ʿa – lā khay–ri'l – wa–rā
T.
Bar.
41
T.
des-tined in a dole so dread-ful ṣal – lī ʿa–lā Aḥ – mad Friends as-
T.
Bar.

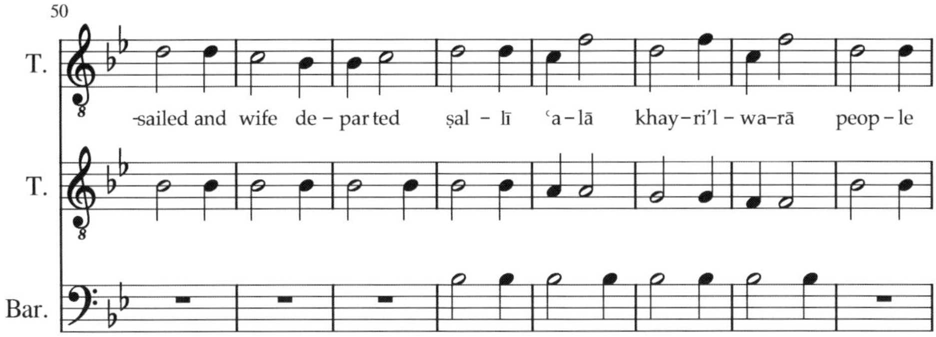
50
T.
-sailed and wife de - par ted ṣal - lī ʿa - lā khay - ri'l - wa - rā peop - le
T.
Bar.

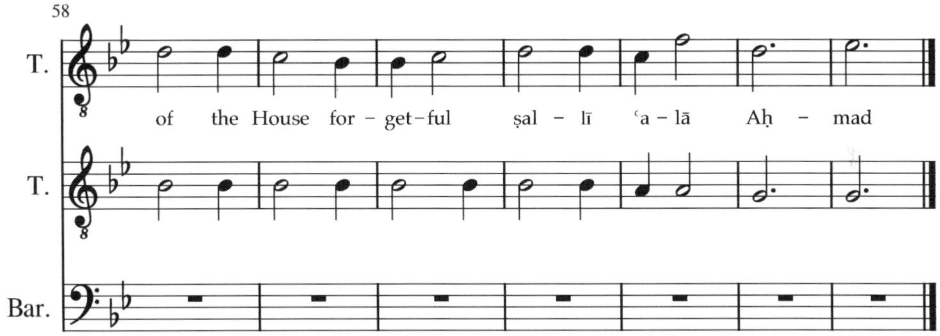
58
T.
of the House for - get - ful ṣal - lī ʿa - lā Aḥ - mad
T.
Bar.

Ṣallī ʿalā khayri'l-warā
Ṣallī ʿalā Aḥmad

1. Years of tears that son of valour
Shed upon the doubting desert
Thorny words and scorning slander
Were the guerdon of his effort

2. Son of sorrows, sum of hardships
Destined in a dole so dreadful
Friends assailed and wife departed
People of the House forgetful

3. In this night of flight surrendered
To the mandate of his Maker
Not for fear of cruel kindred
Nor of venomous lawbreaker

4. Fragrant he, the fearless Prophet
See him stand upon the bedrock
Such a sight of peerless beauty
Manly and of noble bloodstock

5. Now the firmament in darkness
Longs for rise of moon resplendent
Watches, waiting, breath abating
Hushed the heavenly spheres, impendent

6. Comes the hour by Heaven's order
When the dust and stones lamenting
Now the feet of God's Apostle
Feel they not, to God assenting

7. He who made of man a walking
Creature weighed to earth by matter
Able is to wing him higher
Laws confound and reasons scatter

8. Through the layered skies He bears him
Like a lambent lamp nocturnal
Rank on rank of seraphs smiling
Cherished by His hand eternal

Al-taḥiyyātu li'llāhi al-zākiyyātu li'llāhi al-ṭayyibātu'ṣ-ṣalawātu li'Llāh. As-salāmu ʿalayka ayyuha'n-nabiyyu wa-raḥmatu'Llāhi wa-barakātuh. As-salāmu ʿalaynā wa-ʿalā ʿibādillāhi'ṣ-ṣāliḥīn. Ashhadu an lā ilāha illa'Llāh wa-ashhadu anna Muḥammadan ʿabduhu wa-rasūluh

التَّحِيَّاتُ لِلّٰهِ الزَّاكِيَّاتُ لِلّٰهِ الطَّيِّبَاتُ الصَّلَوَاتُ لِلّٰهِ السَّلَامُ عَلَيْكَ أَيُّهَا النَّبِيُّ
وَرَحْمَةُ اللهِ وَبَرَكَاتُهُ السَّلَامُ عَلَيْنَا وَعَلَى عِبَادِ اللهِ الصَّالِحِينَ أَشْهَدُ أَنْ لَا إِلٰهَ إِلَّا
اللهُ وَحْدَهُ لَا شَرِيكَ لَهُ وَأَشْهَدُ أَنَّ مُحَمَّدًا عَبْدُهُ وَرَسُولُهُ

Rising Degrees

انشودة في منازل العروج

Tune: Beauty Deas an Oileáin

يَا رَبَّنَا صَلِّ عَلَى خَيْرِ دَاعٍ لِلّٰهِ

يَا رَبَّنَا صَلِّ عَلَى خَيْرِ دَاعٍ لِلّٰهِ

يَا رَبَّنَا صَلِّ عَلَى خَيْرِ دَاعٍ لِلّٰهِ

صَلِّ يَا رَبِّي وَسَلِّمْ عَلَى خَيْرِ دَاعٍ لِلّٰهِ

Yā Rabbanā ṣallī ʿalā khayri dāʿin li'Llāh
Yā Rabbanā ṣallī ʿalā khayri dāʿin li'Llāh
Yā Rabbanā ṣallī ʿalā khayri dāʿin li'Llāh
Ṣallī yā Rabbī wa-sallim ʿalā khayri dāʿin li'Llāh

Now think on two stars that ascended from earth to on high,
When both of them came to the cardinal gate of the sky,
Where Adam the father of women and men did inquire:
'Whom do you bring that would open the gate and so boldly draw nigh?'

So the angel companion responded and thus did reply:
'I bring thy most chosen descendent the Truth to descry!
Muḥammad, the praised and the praising, to heaven doth fly.'
'Has he been sent?' was the question; the glorious answer was 'Aye'.

They passed through the portal and unto the next gate drew nigh.
That question was asked and again came the angel's reply;
The door did fly wide and they Yaḥyā and Christ did espy:
'Welcome, o welcome; thy coming is good!' did the two prophets cry.

Rejoicing they watched the fair mount of Muḥammad pass by,
The third of those gates then was opened a light to supply.
Fair Joseph, one half of all beauty, stood there and did cry:
'Welcome my brother, thou prophet, for whose noble face lovers sigh.'

Came he forth to the fourth of the heavens his will to comply.
Idrīs the high master of secrets of number and sky.
'O has he been sent?' came his question and then the reply:
'Welcome my brother and prophet, who on hidden truth doth rely.'

Then Gabriel brought the Burāq through the dark of the sky,
They blazed in the blackness and then the fifth door did espy.
'Who has come?' came the voice; it was Aaron the priest who stood by
Heaven's relator; so 'Welcome' bade he to that servant brought nigh.

Then the man who with God was conversant on far Sinai,
God's messenger Moses did magic and Pharoah defy,
Now weeps at the hosts of Muḥammad their multitude high:
'Welcome my brother, your coming is good', hear that lawgiver cry!

Then Gabriel knocked at the portal of that seventh sky.
'Who is there?' came the question. 'Muḥammad' the envoy did cry.
To the Seal of the Prophets his forefather Abraham nigh.
'Welcome, good son and good Prophet!' he said, ''tis the hour to draw nigh.'

The Highest Rank

Reflect, my brothers, on the shining of that pair, Seraph and Seal, as they cast into perfect harmony the city and the sanctuary, Mecca and Jerusalem, old and new, heaven and earth, God and man. Thus is the meed of Ishmael, from whose resting-place did this rising begin. Has so great a journey been, since the elder times? Truly, so did Adam descend, that now Aḥmad might rise up!

On that night all was peace and joy. What was apart was joined together; what was fallen was restored, what was forgotten was called to mind and heart; as a thousand angels praised the majesty of the Sovereign Lord.

But hold it in your thinking, brothers, that our story is not yet complete, and the tale of his mission is as yet unfinished. For now the Chosen One shall travel in a splendour supernal, beyond the confines of the spheres, to the world which is beyond worlds, to the light which is beyond all lights.

How great and sweet a mystery, as the Man of Praise is guided, free of all stain, beyond the elder prophecy itself, into the place of Unity which is the fount of all places!

Al-taḥiyyātu li'llāhi al-zākiyyātu li'llāhi al-ṭayyibātu'ṣ-ṣalawātu li'Llāh.
As-salāmu ʿalayka ayyuha'n-nabiyyu wa-raḥmatu'Llāhi wa-barakātuh.
As-salāmu ʿalaynā wa-ʿalā ʿibādillāhi'ṣ-ṣāliḥīn. Ashhadu an lā ilāha
illa'Llāh wa-ashhadu anna Muḥammadan ʿabduhu wa-rasūluh

التَّحِيَّاتُ لِلَّهِ الزَّاكِيَّاتُ لِلَّهِ الطَّيِّبَاتُ الصَّلَوَاتُ لِلَّهِ السَّلَامُ عَلَيْكَ أَيُّهَا النَّبِيُّ
وَرَحْمَةُ اللهِ وَبَرَكَاتُهُ السَّلَامُ عَلَيْنَا وَعَلَى عِبَادِ اللهِ الصَّالِحِينَ أَشْهَدُ أَنْ لَا إِلَهَ إِلَّا
اللهُ وَحْدَهُ لَا شَرِيكَ لَهُ وَأَشْهَدُ أَنَّ مُحَمَّدًا عَبْدُهُ وَرَسُولُهُ

Litany XXXII

صلوات شريفة

أَعُوذُ بِٱللَّهِ مِنَ ٱلشَّيۡطَٰنِ ٱلرَّجِيمِ

بِسۡمِ ٱللَّهِ ٱلرَّحۡمَٰنِ ٱلرَّحِيمِ

وَٱلنَّجۡمِ إِذَا هَوَىٰ ١ مَا ضَلَّ صَاحِبُكُمۡ وَمَا غَوَىٰ ٢
وَمَا يَنطِقُ عَنِ ٱلۡهَوَىٰٓ ٣ إِنۡ هُوَ إِلَّا وَحۡيٞ يُوحَىٰ ٤
عَلَّمَهُۥ شَدِيدُ ٱلۡقُوَىٰ ٥ ذُو مِرَّةٖ فَٱسۡتَوَىٰ ٦ وَهُوَ
بِٱلۡأُفُقِ ٱلۡأَعۡلَىٰ ٧ ثُمَّ دَنَا فَتَدَلَّىٰ ٨ فَكَانَ قَابَ قَوۡسَيۡنِ
أَوۡ أَدۡنَىٰ ٩ فَأَوۡحَىٰٓ إِلَىٰ عَبۡدِهِۦ مَآ أَوۡحَىٰ ١٠ مَا كَذَبَ
ٱلۡفُؤَادُ مَا رَأَىٰٓ ١١ أَفَتُمَٰرُونَهُۥ عَلَىٰ مَا يَرَىٰ ١٢ وَلَقَدۡ
رَءَاهُ نَزۡلَةً أُخۡرَىٰ ١٣ عِندَ سِدۡرَةِ ٱلۡمُنتَهَىٰ ١٤ عِندَهَا
جَنَّةُ ٱلۡمَأۡوَىٰٓ ١٥ إِذۡ يَغۡشَى ٱلسِّدۡرَةَ مَا يَغۡشَىٰ ١٦ مَا
زَاغَ ٱلۡبَصَرُ وَمَا طَغَىٰ ١٧ لَقَدۡ رَأَىٰ مِنۡ ءَايَٰتِ رَبِّهِ
ٱلۡكُبۡرَىٰٓ ١٨

Wondrous Oneness

أنشودة الحيرة عند مشاهدة الوحدة

Tune: Mo rùn geal, dìleas

صَلِّ يَا رَبِّي عَلَى مُحَمَّد صَلِّ يَا رَبِّي عَلَى النَّبِي
صَلِّ يَا رَبِّي عَلَى مُحَمَّد وَكُلِّ الآلِ مَعَ الصَّحْبِ

Ṣallī yā Rabbī ʿalā Muḥammad, ṣallī yā Rabbī ʿala'n-nabī
Ṣallī yā Rabbī ʿalā Muḥammad, wa-kulli'l-āli maʿa'ṣ-ṣaḥbi

1. And so did Aḥmad, the only Prophet
To carry warrant to enter there,
Surpass the skies and the higher heavens
His shining spirit in praise and prayer.

2. And in that station the fairest man to
The Peopled Mansion now did repair:
The serried angels rose to salute him:
O blessed hero beyond compare!

3. And then beholding two running rivers
Which worldly rivals may seek to share.
And then beyond them two further waters
To which the holiest hosts repair.

4. O see him now, opening his heart's eye
To see the Tree of the Ending there,
The Chosen Man, by God's glory gladdened,
Did pristine pure unity declare.

5. And at Two Bows' Lengths that holy Prophet
Or 'nearer still' as the books declare,
A mystery of the wondrous oneness
His heart did know, perfectly aware.

6. Three chalices from the seraph shining
Were his to choose and his choice declare.
Now see the choice of the wise Muḥammad,
The milk was meet for his nature fair.

7. Let Adam's children ferment relinquish
All fevers which must the heart impair;
Let all be free of all worldly whiling
Of earthly honey let us beware.

(*the milk is served*) لَا إِلٰهَ إِلَّا اللّٰه

8. Then as the lote-tree in gold was shrouded
The Lord for Aḥmad did gifts prepare:
Three shining verses, and for the sinful
Forgiveness, and then the grace of prayer.

9. And therefore know, all my loving brethren,
He at the End shall all honour wear.
So bless him, hope for his intercession,
And let your heartbeats his name declare.

The Lote Tree

Alone did he travel, where Gabriel could not pass, into the final rank and unity, where the lote-tree was shrouded in mystery, where his holy eye neither swerved nor erred, to receive the cup of nature, and then three golden gifts. The mind is dazzled and quails before such majesty and glory! The secret of Unity itself was unveiled before his sight, and he knew truly through the witnessing of his heart the truth of *Lā ilāha illa'Llāh.*

And he knew the truth of *Lā ḥawla wa-lā quwwata illā bi'Llāh.*
And he knew the truth of *Lā ghāliba illa'Llāh.*
And he knew the truth of *Ḥasbuna'Llāh.*
And the angels did say, as we say:

Al-taḥiyyātu li'llāhi al-zākiyyātu li'llāhi al-ṭayyibātu'ṣ-ṣalawātu li'Llāh.
As-salāmu ʿalayka ayyuha'n-nabiyyu wa-raḥmatu'Llāhi wa-barakātuh.
As-salāmu ʿalaynā wa-ʿalā ʿibādillāhi'ṣ-ṣāliḥīn. Ashhadu an lā ilāha illa'Llāh wa-ashhadu anna Muḥammadan ʿabduhu wa-rasūluh

التَّحِيَّاتُ لِلّٰهِ الزَّاكِيَّاتُ لِلّٰهِ الطَّيِّبَاتُ الصَّلَوَاتُ لِلّٰهِ السَّلَامُ عَلَيْكَ أَيُّهَا النَّبِيُّ
وَرَحْمَةُ اللهِ وَبَرَكَاتُهُ السَّلَامُ عَلَيْنَا وَعَلَى عِبَادِ اللهِ الصَّالِحِينَ أَشْهَدُ أَنْ لَا إِلٰهَ إِلَّا
اللهُ وَحْدَهُ لَا شَرِيكَ لَهُ وَأَشْهَدُ أَنَّ مُحَمَّدًا عَبْدُهُ وَرَسُولُهُ

The Litany of the Glories

صلاة السبحات

Tune: Hugh Kelly

١

صَلِّ رَبِّي عَلَى أَحْمَد
صَلِّ رَبِّي عَلَى أَحْمَد
مَنْ سَرَى فِي لَيْلَةٍ
بِرِفْقَةِ خَيرِالمَلَايِكَةِ الأَمِين

صَلِّ رَبِّي عَلَى أَحْمَد
صَلِّ رَبِّي عَلَى أَحْمَد
مَا طَغَى الفُؤَادُ لَمَّا
قَارَبَ المَقَامَ الأَسْنَى
خَتْمُ المُرْسَلِين

٢

صَلِّ رَبِّي عَلَى أَحْمَد
صَلِّ رَبِّي عَلَى أَحْمَد
سَامِعٍ صَدَى الأَقْلَامِ
سَمْعًا مُعجِزَ الأَنَامِ
خَتْمُ المُرْسَلِين

صَلِّ رَبِّي عَلَى أَحْمَد
صَلِّ رَبِّي عَلَى أَحْمَد
ثَمَّةَ رُؤْيَةُ الأَلْوَانِ
ثُمَّ نَارًا وَالجِنَانِ
خَتْمُ المُرْسَلِين

The Five Prayers

And so give thanks, friends gathered here,
    and take this gift from Heaven's Lord,
In grace and glory gifted us,
    from Him to us a binding cord.

From purest place and highest King,
    and greatest man that ever soared
beyond this world of trial and tears,
    we reap this rite as his reward.

The Year of Sorrow ended when
    the Man of Praise his King adored.
No purer joy adorns the heart
    when love's red wine is freely poured.

And we poor mortals caught in grief
    in this base world of sham and fraud
are offered now this Zamzam cup
    to clean the souls that demons clawed.

At dawn we cry for holiness,
    for freedom from our egos flawed,
at noon we turn away from bread
    and bend our hearts to heaven's hoard.

Midafternoon, at dusk and dark,
    we follow him and turn toward
the Primal House, where prophets prayed
    and holy souls arose and soared.

Released from hour and place we face
    the Face the purest ones adored.
In unity we sing His song:
    the heart lies not, the soul's restored!

The Prophets and the holy men
    shall hold our hands, with one accord
in grace they upward guide our gaze,
    until in God we are restored.

Litany XXIV

صلوات شريفة

Tune: Bó Na Leath Adhairce

Nation, Rejoice!

أنشودة احتفال الأمة المحمدية

وَصَلَّى اللهُ عَلَى مَنْ
بِنُورٍ كَمَالِي
بِالحَيِّ حَيِّ قَادَنَا
لِلحَقِّ الأَجْمَلِ

Wa-ṣalla'Llāh ʿalā man
Bi-nūrin kamālī
Bi'l-ḥayyi ḥayyi qādanā
Li'l-ḥaqqi'l-ajmalī

1. Now by this rite united
By mountain, plain and sea,
Our hearts to God are plighted
For all eternity.

2. Where once were men benighted
By evil tyranny
The torch of truth was lighted
Through grace of Prophecy.

3. The Chosen One was flighted
Beyond where sight may see;
By miracle sharp-sighted
Returned with treasures three.

4. That friend from God recited
The signs of Unity,
By them our hearts are righted
From selfhood set us free.

5. And so are we invited
As brethren now to be;
To be in God delighted
As one community.

6. Our prayers by God requited
In far eternity:
Behold us now united
In blessed amity.

7. One day we'll stand clear-sighted
Our wretched works to see;
We pray for hearts united
When he cries 'Ummati!'

بِسۡمِ ٱللَّهِ ٱلرَّحۡمَٰنِ ٱلرَّحِيمِ

لِّلَّهِ مَا فِي ٱلسَّمَٰوَٰتِ وَمَا فِي ٱلۡأَرۡضِۗ وَإِن
تُبۡدُواْ مَا فِيٓ أَنفُسِكُمۡ أَوۡ تُخۡفُوهُ
يُحَاسِبۡكُم بِهِ ٱللَّهُۖ فَيَغۡفِرُ لِمَن يَشَآءُ
وَيُعَذِّبُ مَن يَشَآءُۗ وَٱللَّهُ عَلَىٰ كُلِّ شَيۡءٖ
قَدِيرٌ ٢٨٤

ءَامَنَ ٱلرَّسُولُ بِمَآ أُنزِلَ إِلَيۡهِ مِن
رَّبِّهِۦ وَٱلۡمُؤۡمِنُونَۚ كُلٌّ ءَامَنَ بِٱللَّهِ
وَمَلَٰٓئِكَتِهِۦ وَكُتُبِهِۦ وَرُسُلِهِۦ لَا
نُفَرِّقُ بَيۡنَ أَحَدٖ مِّن رُّسُلِهِۦۚ وَقَالُواْ
سَمِعۡنَا وَأَطَعۡنَاۖ غُفۡرَانَكَ رَبَّنَا
وَإِلَيۡكَ ٱلۡمَصِيرُ ٢٨٥

لَا يُكَلِّفُ ٱللَّهُ نَفۡسًا إِلَّا وُسۡعَهَاۚ
لَهَا مَا كَسَبَتۡ وَعَلَيۡهَا مَا
ٱكۡتَسَبَتۡۗ رَبَّنَا لَا تُؤَاخِذۡنَآ إِن
نَّسِينَآ أَوۡ أَخۡطَأۡنَاۚ رَبَّنَا وَلَا تَحۡمِلۡ
عَلَيۡنَآ إِصۡرٗا كَمَا حَمَلۡتَهُۥ عَلَى
ٱلَّذِينَ مِن قَبۡلِنَاۚ رَبَّنَا وَلَا تُحَمِّلۡنَا
مَا لَا طَاقَةَ لَنَا بِهِۦۖ وَٱعۡفُ عَنَّا
وَٱغۡفِرۡ لَنَا وَٱرۡحَمۡنَآۚ أَنتَ مَوۡلَىٰنَا
فَٱنصُرۡنَا عَلَى ٱلۡقَوۡمِ ٱلۡكَٰفِرِينَ ٢٨٦

Concluding Prayer

اللّٰهُمَّ اجْعَلْنَا مِمَّنْ طَهَّرْتَ لَهُمُ القُلُوبَ وَفَتَحْتَ لَهُمْ أَبْوَابَ الغُيُوبِ وسَتَرْتَ
لَهُمْ قَبَائِحَ العُيُوبَ وَوَهَبْتَ لَهُمْ خيرَ مِنْحَةٍ وَأَجْمَلَ مَوْهُوبٍ

اللّٰهُمَّ عَالِمَ الغيبِ وَالشَّهادَةِ ◉ فَاطِرَ السَّمَوَاتِ وَالأَرْضِ ◉ رَبَّ كُلِّ شَيءٍ
وَمَلِيكَهُ ◉ نَشْهَدُ أَنْ لَا إِلَهَ إِلاَّ أَنْتَ ◉ وَأَنَّ مُحَمَّدًا عَبْدُكَ وَرَسُولُكَ

اللّٰهُمَّ رَبَّ السَّمَوَاتِ السَّبْع وَرَبَّ العَرْشِ العَظِيمِ رَبَّنَا وَرَبَّ كُلِّ شَيءٍ ◉ أَنْتَ
الظَاهِرُ فَلَيسَ فَوقَكَ شَيءٌ وَأَنْتَ البَاطِنُ فَلَيس دُونَكَ شَيءٌ مُنْزِلَ التَّوراةِ
وَالإِنْجِيلِ وَالفُرْقَانِ فَالِقَ الحَبِّ وَالنَّوَى نَعُوذُ بِكَ مِنْ شَرِّ كُلِّ شَيءٍ أَنْتَ آخِذٌ
بِنَاصِيَتِهِ ◉ أَنْتَ الأَوَّلُ فَلَيسَ قَبْلَكَ شَيءٌ وَأَنْتَ الآخِرُ فَلَيس بَعْدَكَ شَيءٌ
اِقْضِ عَنَّا الدَّينَ وَاَغْنِنَا مِنَ الفَقْرِ

Our Lord, by the grace of this gathering and the memory of the Miʿrāj, grant us forgiveness and fair fortune, health in mind and in body, freedom from all that pollutes the soul, and bestow upon us the beauty of loving acceptance of Your decree.

Grant us that we shall not despair when misfortunes assail us with their shadowy oppression. Open our minds to the knowledge of Your goodness and of Your power to bring us out of sorrow by Your blessed road to purity and joy. Liberate us from reliance upon any earthly power or promise.

On this night open our spirits to full love of You, and love of what pleases You, and love of what brings us closer to You; make the love of You more beloved to us than all the treasures of the world, that we may live out our lives in generosity, in fellowship and in hope. Pour out upon our needy hearts the love of Your Chosen One, upon whom be blessings and peace. Render us sincere in his adherence, grant us strength to know and follow his way. Banish from our hearts all unworthy wishes and purify them so that they may mirror perfection alone. Grant us a Burāq of love that we may rise above the lower shadows and approach the dazzling pure light of Your Truth.

And we ask you, O Lord of the Worlds, to grant us the blessing of the intercession of the Chosen One on the last day, that will protect us from all chastisement. May we stand beneath his banner and drink from his fountain of renewing life. Make heavy the balance of our good deeds, grant us to cross the Ṣirāṭ with a speed greater than the speed of a lightning-shaft. May we, though unworthy, know the high blessing of the companionship of the Chosen One in the world which is to come, and the company of the saints and true ones who gave their lives to You.

وَصَلِّ اللّٰهُمَّ عَلَى سَيِّدِنَا وَمَولَانَا مُحَمَّدٍ ذٰلِكَ السِّرَاجِ الوَهَّاجِ ◉ صَاحِبِ الحُلَّةِ
والتَّاجِ ◉ المَخْصُوصِ بِالخُلُقِ العَظِيمِ وَخَتْمِ الرُسُلِ ذِى المِعْرَاجِ ◉ وَعَلَى آلِهِ
وَأَتْبَاعِهِ السَّالِكِينَ عَلَى أَجْمَلِ مِنْهَاجٍ ◉ فَأَعْظِمِ اللّٰهُمَّ بِهِ سُبُلَ نُجُمِ الإِسْلَامِ
وَمَصَابِيحَ الْظَّلَامِ الْمُهْتَدَى بِهِمْ فِى ظُلْمَةِ لَيلِ الشَّكِّ الدَّاجِ ◉ صَلَاةً دَابِمَةً
مُسْتَمِرَّةً مَا تَلَاطَمَتْ فِى الأَبْحُرِ الأَمْوَاجُ وَطَافَ بِالبَيتِ العَتِيقِ مِنْ كُلِّ فَجٍّ
عَمِيقٍ الحُجَّاجُ ◉ وَبَارِكْ لَنَا دَابِمًا فِى الأَوْلَادِ والأَزْوَاجِ

وَاجْعَلْنَا يَا مَولَانَا مِنَ المُحِبِّينَ الصَادِقِينَ لِهٰذَا النَّبِى السِّرَاجِ ◉ الذَّابِقِينَ
بِقِصَّةِ عُرُوجِهِ كَمَالَ السّعَادَةِ وَالاِبْتِهَاجِ ◉ وَأْذَنِ اللّٰهُمَّ بِهذِهِ التِلَاوَةِ المُبَارَكَةِ
كُلَّ كَرْبٍ بِانْفِرَاجِ ◉ وَلَا تُخَيِّبْ آمَالَ عَاكِفٍ عَلَى بَابِكَ مُحْسِنٍ ظَنَّهُ بِكَ رَاجٍ

اللّٰهُمَّ تَقَبَّلْ مِنَّا ◉ اللّٰهُمَّ تَقَبَّلْ مِنَّا ◉ اللّٰهُمَّ تَقَبَّلْ مِنَّا

آمِين

Notes

p.5 Translation of sūra 1: '*Praise is for God, Lord of the Worlds. The Compassionate, the Merciful. King of Judgement-day. Guide us to the straight path; the path of those whom You have blessed, not those upon whom there is wrath, nor those who are gone astray.*'
Translation of sūra 17:1: '*Glory be to He Who brought by night His servant from the Sacred Mosque to the Further Mosque, whose environs We have blessed, that We might show him some of Our signs. Truly He is the All-Hearing, the All-Seeing.*' The Further Mosque is the sanctuary of Jerusalem.
p.8 'Nightingale of Purity'. This preliminary chant is based on an early section of the *Miʿrājiyya* of Ismāʿīl Ḥaqqī Bursevī, and is included to give a flavour of the traditional themes present in *Miʿrāj* recitations. It seeks to evoke the atmosphere of Paradise, thus awakening humanity's natural nostalgia for Eden, which in turn helps us to make sense of the tribulations and fleeting substance of our lives, and our sad intuition that we are far from home. It goes on to indicate the poet's own longing for the Abode of Peace, and the Holy Prophet's ﷺ majestic role in reconciling humanity to nature and to its Lord, through the path of beauty, love and purity. Ṭāhā is one of the Prophet's ﷺ names, and he is also named *al-Muṣṭafā*, the Chosen One, and is hence the appropriate candidate for the unique Ascension.

A hadith narrated by Tirmidhī indicates that 'I was a prophet when Adam was still between water and clay'. In his ultimate nature he is the ancient principle of balance and light, the natural bridgebuilder between creation and Creator. He is humanity in its pure and primal form, reflecting all qualities of perfection, both the Rigorous and the Beautiful.
p.9 Ṭūbā is the spreading tree of Paradise mentioned in the Qur'an (13:39). According to a hadith, a rider would not be able to cross the area of its shade, even in a hundred years.
p.10 'Adam's Descent' is based on a passage by Aḥmad Samʿānī (d.1140) in his *Comfort of the Spirits (Rawḥ al-arwāḥ)*.
p.12 English translation of 'The Prophetic Endurance': 'Take a lesson, brothers, from the Chosen One's endurance, in a year which had passed full of tribulation. Sorrows and the pains of rejection followed one upon the other, and his tears fell for the death of his faithful spouse. It is the lot of the Prophets, who are the folk of patience and purity, to suffer rejection from deniers. Of all people they are tried the most stringently, enduring a misfortune which is unconcealed, issuing from the stubborn, the rejectors,

and the hard of heart. Among the Prophets was Zachariah, upon whose neck the sword fell. The son of Noah also denied his guidance. And when Moses was mocked, he made his Lord his sufficiency. Jesus was hurt by his people with all kinds of repudiation. The Prophets came with guidance and healing. Their hearts were adorned with fidelity. And God was with the patient, openly or in secret, until a Seal came to them with the advent of the Chosen One.'

p.13 'Tahlīl al-Qalādina' means 'the Caledonian Recital of God's Unity'.

p.14 The holy sanctuary is the mosque of Mecca. The Cube of Heaven is the Holy Ka'ba. The First Covenant was the declaration by all souls of God's Lordship at the beginning of creation, described in Qur'an 7:172. The Year of Sadness was the tenth year of the Hijra, when the persecution by idol-worshippers against the fledgling Muslim community in Mecca was at its height, and when Khadīja, the beloved wife of the Prophet ﷺ, and his uncle Abū Ṭālib, both died.

p.16 In a single night, the Burāq carried the Prophet ﷺ miraculously from Mecca to Jerusalem. Jerusalem is the place where the angel Isrāfīl (Seraphiel) will blow the Last Trump, to summon all people to judgement. The ancient temple of Solomon had been converted by the Byzantine emperors into a refuse-heap, on the grounds that Christ was the new temple, and the old site was now the repudiated relic of an Old Covenant. With the arrival of Islam, the city and the sanctuary were revived and adorned. To this day the location of the *Miʿrāj* is indicated by the Dome of the Rock, the first achievement of Islamic architecture.

The 'maid of matriarchs' is the Blessed Virgin Mary, whose giving birth beneath the palm-tree is narrated in sūra 19, which provides the principal inscription within the Dome of the Rock.

p.17 Reaching the mosque of Jerusalem, the Prophet ﷺ affirms the great prophets of previous epochs, and leads them in a harmonious and united prayer to the One God. The mosque is now the 'house of prayer for all nations' foretold in earlier scriptures (Isaiah 56:7), as many ethnic groups were to come on pilgrimage there from around the world, and racial inheritance would be transcended. The Prophet is the 'Seal' (*khatm, khātam*) who affirms and consummates the ancient monotheistic message and its eternal virtues. He is also understood to be the Paraclete, the 'comforter' foretold by Jesus according to earlier accounts (John 14:16), who would 'lead humanity to all truth'. The scene is one of entire inclusion, affirmation, and joy.

p.18 'Star of his Heartland'. This poem indicates that the revival of the Jerusalem sanctuary (*al-Ḥaram al-Sharīf*) takes humanity beyond the old age of priesthood and large-scale animal sacrifice in the Temple. All parts of the sanctuary will now be open to all races and both genders. Gilded splendour and intricate ritual will be replaced by the simple holiness of the prayers brought by the Seal. This is the charism of Ishmael, Abraham's elder son, whose name means 'God has heard', and in whom the Egyptian, and therefore gentile, blood is fused, indicating that through Ishmael's descendent, the Prophet of Islam ﷺ, all humanity is invited to a place of final unity. The Night Journey begins in the semicircular Ḥijr enclosure beside the Ka'ba, which is the burial-place of Ishmael; thus is the symmetry completed.

p.22 Despite suffering untold persecution, the Seal ﷺ concludes his worship together with the souls of the earlier prophets. In the mysterious company of the angels, he rises from the Rock, which is thus ennobled by this symbol of unity and harmony, as the vertical axis intersects with the horizontal unity of the tribes of mankind in Islam. The Dome of the Rock points to Heaven, but also to the four cardinal points of the compass.

p.25 This song rehearses some of the details given in well-known hadiths about the Ascension. Accompanied by the Angel Gabriel, the Prophet ﷺ rises to pass through the seven heavens, in each of which they greet and affirm earlier prophetic sages. Yaḥyā is the biblical John, precursor of Christ. Idrīs, sometimes identified with Enoch, is a prophet to whom esoteric knowledge of the symmetries of creation, in time and number, is attributed. The sound hadiths indicate that Moses weeps with joy when he realizes how numerous will be the followers of the Seal ﷺ.

p.28 Qur'an 53:1-18. The meaning is: '*In the name of God, Compassionate and Merciful. By the star when it sets. Your companion errs not, neither is he misled. He speaks not from caprice. It is nought but a revelation inspired. Taught him by one mighty in strength. Majestic, he grew clear to view. When he was upon the highest horizon. Then he drew nigh and came close. And he was the distance of two bows' lengths, or nearer still. And then He revealed to his servant what He revealed. The heart belied not that which it saw. Do you dispute with him in what he beheld? And he saw him at another descent. At the Lote-tree of the Boundary. Where the Garden of Refuge is. When the Lote-tree was covered by that which covered it. The eye strayed not, neither did it overstep the limit. He saw, of the signs of his Lord, the greatest.*'

p.30 The 'Peopled Mansion' is *al-bayt al-ma'mūr* (Qur'an 52:4), so-called because a hadith tells us that it is visited by seventy thousand angels every day who turn around it (*tawāf*). It is said to be located directly 'above' the Holy Ka'ba, in the seventh heaven; it is the Ka'ba of Heaven.

In the hadiths, Gabriel describes four rivers of Paradise. Two are 'apparent': the Nile and the Euphrates. One of their meanings may be that they have a foundational role in blessing the establishment of human civilization and show how true religion can generate holiness even in the context of developed urban cultures, highlighting the triumph of Moses over Pharoah, and Abraham over Nimrod; while two are 'hidden', being exclusively Paradisal.

The 'Tree of the Ending', or 'Lote Tree of the Ending', is the *sidrat al-muntahā* mentioned in the above Qur'anic passage. It is said to be the point where the branching ramification of the world vanishes into pure Unity.

'Two Bows' Lengths'. Again this is Qur'anic (53:9). It may refer to the ancient royal practice of not permitting a guest to come closer than this distance to a king; or it may signify 'great proximity' in a general way; or the point at which the descent and ascent of Being commences and ends, in two great 'arcs' (*qawsayn*).

'Three chalices': according to the hadith, at this exalted place, Gabriel offers the Seal ﷺ three cups: of honey, wine and milk. He chooses the milk, and is told: 'You have been guided to the *fiṭra*': the primordial natural disposition of man. Islam is to be the spiritual way of those seeking harmony with nature, so frequently invoked in the Qur'anic text.

'in gold was shrouded': according to some hadiths, the Sidra was mysteriously covered in gold, the colour of imperishability. The gold of the Dome of the Rock is sometimes believed to hint at this mystery.

'three shining verses': sūra 2 verses 284-6 were granted to the Chosen One ﷺ at this time. See page 38.

'forgiveness and then the grace of prayer'. The Holy Prophet ﷺ receives the right of the supreme intercession (*shafā'a*) for grave sinners, and the five daily prayers of Islam are bestowed.

p.31 *Lā ḥawla wa-lā quwwata illā bi'Llāh:* 'There is neither power nor strength save by God.'

Lā ghāliba illa'Llāh: 'God alone is Victorious'.

Ḥasbuna'Llāh: 'God is our sufficiency'.

p.33 Translation: (verse 1): 'My Lord, bless Aḥmad, who voyaged by night in the company of the best Angel, the Trustworthy. My Lord, bless Aḥmad, whose heart did not stray when he neared the Highest Station, Seal of the Messengers. (verse 2): My Lord, bless Aḥmad, who heard the sound of the pens, in a miraculous way impossible for other men, Seal of the Messengers. My Lord, bless Aḥmad; there he beheld the colours, and then the Fire and the Gardens. Seal of the Messengers.'

'The sound of the pens'. The hadith record the mystery of how the Man of Praise heard the pens writing the destiny of the world.

'He beheld the colours'. The Lote Tree was 'covered with colours; what they were I do not know.'

'The Fire and the Gardens'. During his ascension the Prophet ﷺ was granted a vision of Hell and Heaven. This narrative is believed to have found its way through Muslim Spain to Dante, forming the basis of his *Divine Comedy*.

p.34 'The Five Prayers'. One of the three holy gifts granted the Seal ﷺ in the divine presence was the *ṣalāt*, which literally means 'the Link', the five-times-daily formal worship, whose five times are indicated in this poem. The hadith report that the initial gift was of fifty prayers in each day, but that Moses told the Man of Praise ﷺ that his people would not be able to sustain such a duty; the Man of Praise then returned to his Lord, and received successive reductions, until, when the number reached five, he felt shy to return again to ask for a further dispensation. Then, decisively establishing the Prayer, a herald cried out, in God's name: 'I have executed the obligation I have decreed, and I have made the burden light for My servants'. Islam is to be the religion in which the heavy load imposed upon earlier communities is lifted (Qur'an 7:157); the Holy Prophet proclaims: 'Make matters easy, not hard; give good news, and do not repel people.' Those Muslims in decadent times who insist on the more burdensome interpretations risk denying this distinctive quality of the Final Religion.

The Five Prayers of Islam are thus the daily recollection of the Ascension, an opportunity to turn toward the earthly symbol of the Divine eternity, so that with one's heart one rises from worldly distractions towards the Abode of Purity.

p.37 This song relates the Seal's ﷺ ineffable journey to our own situation. Only by approaching the Divine will we know holiness, and hence liberation from lower impulses. As we stand shoulder-to-shoulder, we begin to experience the miracle of the unity of all believers, who stand together and equally before the Divine Mystery. With hearts lovingly united to God and to each other, we may hope to receive the Prophetic Intercession, when, on the Last Day, the Man of Praise goes before the Divine throne, and prostrates himself, saying: '*ummatī, ummatī*': 'My community! My community!' Through this mediation will countless men and women be saved.

p.38 Here we have the three verses gifted to the Chosen One ﷺ during his Ascent. The translation runs: '*In the name of God, the Compassionate and Merciful. To God belongs all that is in the heavens and the earth. If you reveal what is in your selves, or hide it, God shall still call you to account for it. And He will forgive whomsoever He wills, and punish whomsoever He wills. And God is over all things Powerful. The Messenger believes in what is revealed to him from his Lord, as do the* *believers. Each believes in God, and His angels, and His books and Messengers. We make no distinction between any one of His messengers. And they say: We hear and we obey! Your forgiveness, Lord! And to You is the journeying. God does not charge a soul with anything beyond its capacity. What it acquired is to its credit, and what it gained is to its discredit. Our Lord, do not take us to task if we forget or slip! Our Lord! Do not impose upon us a burden as You imposed it upon those who came before us. Our Lord! Do not impose upon us that which is beyond our strength! Forgive us and pardon us, and show us mercy. You are our Lord, so give us victory against the unbelieving folk.'*

p.40 The Ṣirāṭ is the bridge which spans Hell, over which all must pass at the end of time as a visible sign of God's judgement.